D0538745

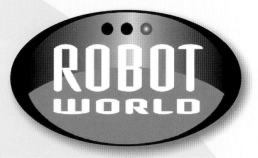

Robots in Fiction and Films

by Steve Parker

amicus

Published by Amicus
P.O. Box 1329
Mankato, MN 56002

Printed in the United States of America, at Corporate
Graphics in North Mankato, Minnesota.

Library of Congress Cataloging-in-Publication Data

Parker, Steve, 1952-
  Robots in fiction and films / by Steve Parker.
      p. cm. – (Robot world)
  Includes index.
  Summary: "Discusses how robots are featured in popular
  culture, including films and fiction. Also discusses real
  and imagined advances in robotics, and how realistically
  the technology is represented"–Provided by publisher.
  ISBN 978-1-60753-073-2 (library binding)
  1. Robots–Juvenile literature. 2. Cinematography–Special
effects–Juvenile literature. 3. Science fiction–Juvenile
literature. I. Title.
  TJ211.2.H536 2011
  629.8'92–dc22
                                        2010001125

Created by Appleseed Editions Ltd.
Designed by Guy Callaby
Edited by Mary-Jane Wilkins
Picture research by Su Alexander

Picture acknowledgements
Title page Rune Hellestad/Corbis; contents page ShaunFinch/Alamy;
4 ArcadeImages/Alamy; 5t My Childhood Memories/Alamy, b 20th
Century Fox/CBS Television/The Kobal Collection; 6 Lebrecht Music and
Arts Photo Library/Alamy; 7l UFA/The Kobal Collection, r Paris Pierce/
Alamy; 8 The Protective Art Archive/Alamy; 9t PYMCA/Alamy, b John
Springer Collection/Corbis; 10 Deborah Feingold/Corbis; 11t 20th
Century Fox/The Kobal Collection/Digital Domain, b Getty Images;
12 Photos 12/Alamy; 13l MGM/The Kobal Collection, r Photos
12/Alamy; 14 Interfoto/Alamy; 15t Orion/The Kobal Collection,
b Universal/The Kobal Collection; 15 Hanna-Barbera/The Kobal
Collection; 17 Everett Collection/Rex Features; 18 Warner Brothers/The
Kobal Collection; 19t The Moviestore Collection.com, b Orion/The Kobal
Collection; 20t Touchstone/Spyglass Entertainment/The Kobal Collection,
b Lucasfilm/The Kobal Collection/Hamshere,Keith; 21 Photos 12/Alamy;
22 Amblin/Dreamworks/WB/The Kobal Collection/James, David;
23t Bettmann/Corbis, b Tri-Star/The Kobal Collection; 24 ABC-TV/The
Kobal Collection; 25t Paramount Television/The Kobal Collection,
b ShaunFinch/Alamy; 26 Disney/The Kobal Collection; 27t Carolco/The
Kobal Collection, b 20th Century Fox/The Kobal Collection; 28 Rune
Hellestad/Corbis; 29t Dreamworks/The Kobal Collection, b Lucasfilm/
20th Century Fox/The Kobal Collection
Front cover: 20th Century Fox/The Kobal Collection/Digital Domain

DAD0040
32010

9 8 7 6 5 4 3 2 1

Contents

Robo-stars

Have you seen the latest robot superstars? Their story started as a book, which was turned into a cartoon. Then came the TV series and blockbuster movies. You can buy their robot toys and models, posters and books, lunch boxes and pens. Everyone recognizes the robo-celebrities. See their latest DVD. Watch them on stage. Buy their music and their computer game, too!

That's Entertainment

Who—or what—are these megastar robots? In one sense, it does not matter. Every year or two, a new story starring robots is published. The entertainment business soon starts to make money on them. People watch them on screen, read about them, and buy their products by the millions. Like all famous celebrities, in time they become less popular. But then along comes another story with a new set of robots—and it all happens again.

▼ *In early video and computer games, such as Escape from the Planet of the Robot Monsters (1989), the robots moved stiffly, like old clockwork toys —and so did the people!*

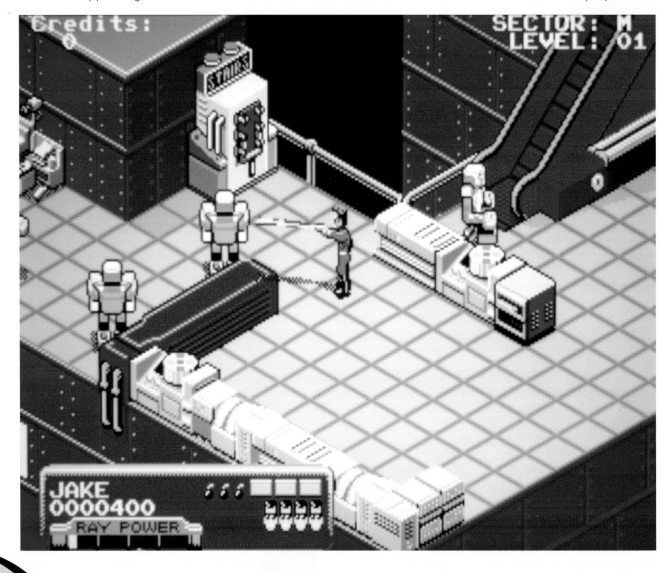

▶▶ *During the 1950s, robots starred in board games, jigsaw puzzles, and similar products. This was well before most people owned computers, video games, remote controllers, or even televisions.*

Make-Believe

Millions of people around the world are fascinated by tales of robots, **cyborgs**, **androids**, and similar imaginary machines. Some of them are good, others are evil. Some are super strong, others are weak. We might have a favorite member of the robot team and imagine we have its amazing powers. We like the good robots to win, while the baddies are beaten. We are fascinated by their stories, in which anything can happen, anywhere, at any time—because it's all fiction, made up and pretend.

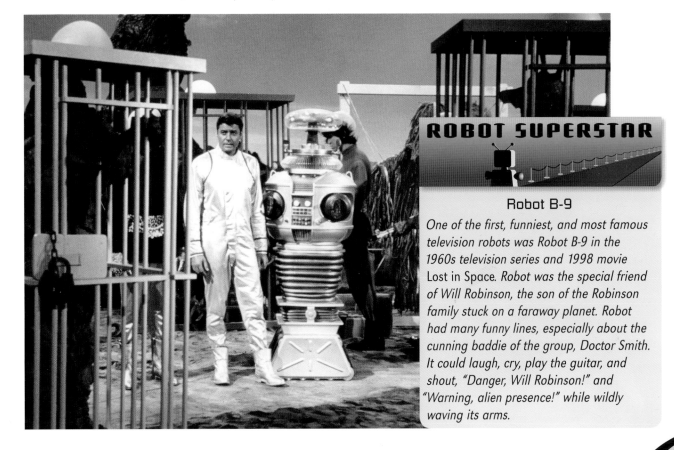

ROBOT SUPERSTAR

Robot B-9

One of the first, funniest, and most famous television robots was Robot B-9 in the 1960s television series and 1998 movie Lost in Space. Robot was the special friend of Will Robinson, the son of the Robinson family stuck on a faraway planet. Robot had many funny lines, especially about the cunning baddie of the group, Doctor Smith. It could laugh, cry, play the guitar, and shout, "Danger, Will Robinson!" and "Warning, alien presence!" while wildly waving its arms.

The Original Robots

The word robot is less than a hundred years old. It came not from science but from fiction. It was invented in 1920 by Czech writer Karel Čapek for his play *RUR (Rossum's Universal Robots)*, first performed in 1921. Karel said that his brother Josef came up with the word while helping him write.

Living Robots

In Čapek's story, the robots were not so much machines as artificial living things. They were designed by people, then their body parts were grown separately and put together in factories. The idea was taken from the car industry, which was growing rapidly at the time. Cars were built by adding parts, one after another on an assembly line. The robots in the story were made in a similar way on a production line but from living parts.

Slaves Fight Back

The word robot was based on the Czech word *robota*, meaning people who were forced to work as slaves. The robots were servants or workers under the control of their human masters. Čapek's play tells how the robots turned against their masters and fought to be free, eventually killing all humans.

◀◀ *Karel Čapek (1890–1938) was a Czech author who wrote fairy tales and detective stories, as well as what we now call science fiction.*

A Change in Meaning

RUR (Rossum's Universal Robots) was a great success around the world, and was made into TV programs and films. The new word robot was short, sharp and sounded good, and it soon caught on. Its meaning changed from being the name of the slave-like beings in the original play. Robot came to mean any machine with moving parts that can do tasks and carry out jobs largely by itself and react to what happens around it, under the overall control of humans.

▲ *In Čapek's play, the robots are not mechanical or electronic, but mostly alive—what today we might call cyborgs. At first they work hard under human control, but that gradually changes.*

ROBO-FUTURE

Maria

The first big movie featuring robots was Metropolis in 1927. This dark story is set in a bleak future city, with a woman-shaped robot, which is the machine-like evil twin of a character called Maria. The special effects were very advanced for their time, showing Maria gradually changing between human and robot forms. The plastic-like robot suit worn by Brigitte Helm, the actress who also played Maria, was very uncomfortable. Sometimes during a long day's filming, she broke down in tears.

Robots Take Off

After the success of the original robots in *RUR (Rossum's Universal Robots)*, many machine-like robots began to appear in stories and fiction. Advances in science, and in designing and building real robots, meant that imaginary robots changed, too.

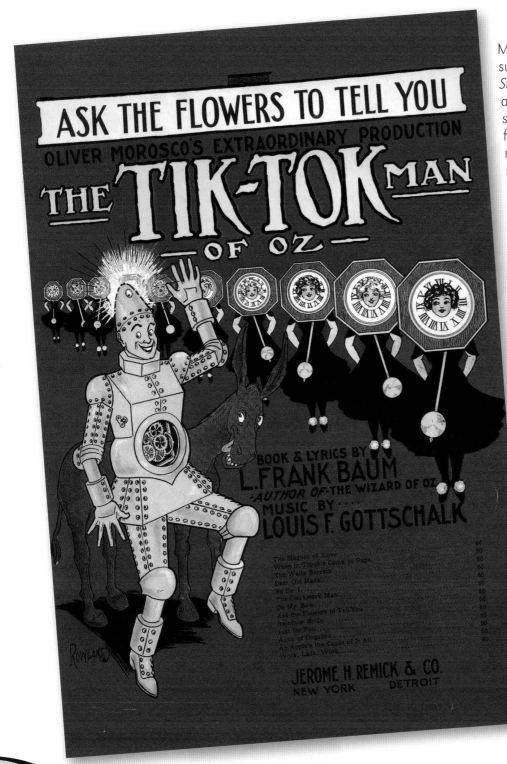

Robots into Space

Many robot films from the 1950s, such as *The Day the Earth Stood Still* (1951), *Robot Monster* (1953), and *The Invisible Boy* (1957), had space as their theme. They featured rockets, flying saucers, ray guns, aliens, and various robots having space adventures. This was partly because, at the time, real-life engineers were building bigger, better rockets to go into space. The space race was on and new frontiers were crossed when the first **satellite**, Sputnik, was launched in 1957 and when the first astronaut, Yuri Gagarin, went into space in 1961.

The fashion for fictional space robots during the 1950s and 1960s shows how the appearance, powers, behavior, and adventures of fictional robots are influenced by real events.

◄◄ *Tik-Tok was a windup mechanical person in the Land of Oz books (1900–1920) by L. Frank Baum, and the Oz plays and movies. Tik-Tok is seen as fiction's first robot, even though the term robot had not been invented.*

When robotic dancing, a dancer moves in a stiff, awkward way, like a machine with levers. Modern fictional robots are much more lifelike movers!

The Age of Androids

Many early fictional robots were androids. They looked similar to a human, with a head, body, arms, and legs. Some of the androids behaved like people, talking and reacting to events around them. But at first they did this in a very limited and mechanical way, to show that they were just machines. As real robots became more complicated and lifelike, so did the imaginary ones.

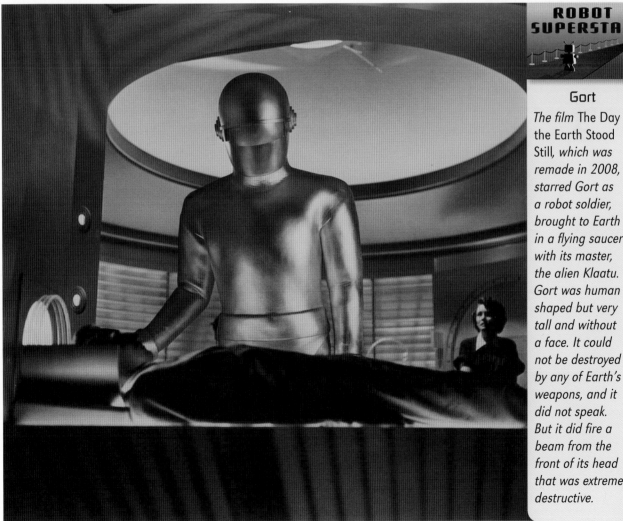

ROBOT SUPERSTAR

Gort

The film The Day the Earth Stood Still, *which was remade in 2008, starred Gort as a robot soldier, brought to Earth in a flying saucer with its master, the alien Klaatu. Gort was human shaped but very tall and without a face. It could not be destroyed by any of Earth's weapons, and it did not speak. But it did fire a beam from the front of its head that was extremely destructive.*

Imaginary Laws

The three laws of robotics are not real laws, but rules invented for a work of fiction: *Runaround*, a short story published in 1942 by **science fiction** writer Isaac Asimov (1920–1992). Asimov wrote hundreds of science fiction stories, including the *I, Robot* series.

What the Laws Say

The first law says that a robot may not harm a human being or, through inaction (not doing something), allow a human to suffer harm.

The second law says that a robot must obey orders given to it by humans, except when these orders go against the first law.

The third law allows a robot to protect itself, so long as this does not conflict with the first or second laws.

Isaac Asimov spent many years writing his Robot and Foundation series, then joined them together in new stories that showed his grand vision of robots and the future.

Back to Zero

In later years Asimov added another law, which he called the zeroth law, meaning it should come before the other three. This law says that a robot may not harm humanity or, by inaction, allow humanity to come to harm. By "humanity" Asimov meant all people, rather than individual humans. Other writers have added more laws since. For example, a robot must always tell people that it is a robot. And even the cleverest robot should know that it is a robot and not a human being.

The laws of robotics are not about technology or engineering. Instead, they look at the actions and behavior of robots, and how they relate to humans. Over the years, they have had a huge effect on the storylines and plots for robot fiction.

◀◀ *Asimov's* I, Robot *series inspired the 2004 movie of the same name. Sonny is one of the most complex NS-5 robots. It joins humans to battle against rogue versions of its own kind.*

ROBOT OR NOT?

The Daleks

The television time-lord, Doctor Who, has battled against the daleks since the 1960s. Daleks look like robots, move on wheels or hover, and speak with robot-like voices. But inside each dalek is a living being, a small, alien creature like a green blob with tentacles. The dalek is a protective, mobile outer shell for the creature, in the same way that humans are mobile and protected inside cars. See page 25 for a photo of another villain from the series.

How Robot Stories Change

Most early stories about robots described them as machines carrying out the will of their human creators. But soon the story plots became more complicated. Some robots were shown as slaves wanting to break free from their human masters. Another idea was that robots had started out as stupid but gradually became more intelligent, so that in the end they became smarter than the people who made them.

Making Decisions

As robots became more common in works of fiction, writers, artists, and filmmakers developed more storylines involving them. Some looked at the way smart robots made decisions about what was good or bad and compared them to the ways in which humans made similar decisions.

Difficult Choices

Sometimes a robot is told to harm humans. It should not do so because this goes against the laws of robotics (see pages 10-11). But what if a human is evil, harming or killing many others? As robot fiction became more complicated, some robots were given humanlike feelings and emotions, such as happiness, sadness, love, and hate.

Major Motoko Kusanagi is a cyborg star in the Kokaku Kidotai *(Ghost in the Shell)* movies, cartoon strips, video games, and novels. She is portrayed as female, unlike most cyborgs, who are muscle-bound males.

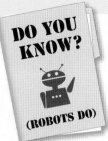

Robbie the Robot

In the 1956 movie Forbidden Planet, *Robbie the Robot had great strength and skill and was very smart. On planet Altai IV, it tried to protect its human masters from a terrible monster.*

But it could not kill this enemy, because the monster was part of the imagination of its human master, Doctor Morbius. The laws of robotics say that robots should not harm people. This story was based on The Tempest, *a play by William Shakespeare.*

Robot Creators

All fictional robots are created by people—writers, artists, model makers, engineers, costume designers, set designers, filmmakers, and others. They imagine what the robots might look like and what they could do. As real science progresses, we can achieve things that 50 years ago seemed impossible. Robot creators follow this progress. Yet the real engineering and technology of fictional robots is not all that important. They are imaginary, so their creators can give them ever-greater strength, speed, cleverness, and undreamed-of powers—it's all make believe.

▶▶ *Robot creators can take any creature, make a machine-like version, and weave it into a story. Bubo the Owl, invented for the 1981 film* Clash of the Titans, *was not in the original ancient Greek myth.*

Real or Pretend?

Some fictional robots in television and films are real in the sense that they exist as actual objects or models, made from plastic, metal, wood, rubber, and other materials. But these robots cannot do everything they do on screen, such as throwing cars around, reading people's minds, or making buildings explode with their ray guns.

Added Extras

For these types of robots, camera crews, audio engineers, **special effects** technicians, and many other experts add all kinds of tricks and extras. They can make a robot appear faster, stronger, smarter, and more dangerous than it really is. For example, a movie-star robot appears to race along at an amazing speed on its whizzing wheels. In fact, the real model version can only trundle along slowly on its wheels. It is filmed, and then the playback is speeded up so it seems to go much faster.

▼ *Mechagodzilla (on the far left) was the robot enemy of superstar giant dino-reptile Godzilla (far right) in films from the 1970s. It was played by actor Wataru Fukuda, wearing a rubber and plastic suit.*

⏵⏵ Since 1987, Robocop has starred in movies, books, comics, video games, and television series. Here one of the many models of the cyborg police officer is prepared for special effects filming (see also page 19).

Outside and Inside

Some of these "real" robots are operated by remote control by a person using radio signals, in the same way as a radio-controlled car or plane. They have electric motors, gears, and levers inside to make them move. Another type of robot is worked from the outside by people using wires or levers, like a puppet. A third technique is for someone inside to work the robot. Big robots may have three or four operators inside, pulling levers and pressing buttons. Being inside a robot machine like this is often cramped and uncomfortable.

Many of the robots from old movies and programs look simple and silly now. But before **computer animation** and **digital special effects**, they impressed millions of viewers.

ROBOT SUPERSTAR

Huey, Dewey, and Louie

These three small robots from the 1972 film Silent Running *accompanied human space worker Lowell, tending trees in an enormous greenhouse spaceship, after all plant life on Earth had died. Lowell trained them to be his friends and do jobs around the ship. Each robot was worked by a person inside who was an* **amputee**—*someone who had lost body parts due to accident or disease. The names Huey, Dewey, and Louie were taken from the three duckling nephews of long-time cartoon hero Donald Duck.*

What Robots Look Like

Model makers building a three-dimensional robot are limited by the materials they use. Even with the best special effects, a real robot can only do so much. But there are no limits to what a robot that exists as only drawings or pictures, on paper or screen, can do.

Scenes and Movements

In comics, books, and animations, nothing exists as real objects. There are no parts made of metal and plastic, just shapes and colors on paper or a screen. Artists and designers can decide what a robot looks like, how it moves and behaves, what appears in the background of each scene, and almost everything else. For example, imagine that a cartoon robot suddenly has to move fast. The artist can change its shape from upright and stiff, to sloping forward and shaking with speed. This gives the impression of fast movement.

Gobots could change or transform from one shape to another. They appeared in the early 1980s. In this scene, the artist uses curling lines to show smoke and fumes. Gobots were soon overtaken by Transformers.

Boy Robot

Astro Boy was an early cartoon robot, first drawn in 1951 by artist and **animator** Osamu Tezuka. This boy robot had laser beams in his fingers, fired rockets from his arms, and could fly. Unlike many robots, Astro Boy showed emotions such as happiness and sadness. He became a star around the world.

How Astro Boy Changed

After appearing in hundreds of comic books, Astro Boy became a television cartoon in the 1960s. At the time, animations were created by people who drew the pictures or **frames** by hand, each one just a tiny bit different from the last. Showing the frames one after the other, many per second, blurred the changes together to give the impression of smooth movements. By 2003, Astro Boy was a computer animation (see pages 18–19).

Robots in Action ▪

ROBO-HOLOGRAMS

Holograms are special pictures taken with laser light. They have the two dimensions of an image on a flat surface, up and down and left to right. They also have the third dimension of depth or distance, front to back. Robots such as Astro Boy have featured in many action-scene hologram pictures in books and on stickers and toys. ▪

⤒ *Astro Boy came from the Japanese comic style known as manga. He was "adopted" as a son by the chief of the Ministry of Science. Astro Boy fights evil and crime—especially crimes committed by other robots.*

Robots and Computers

Before computers, real robots built from parts such as motors and wheels, were mostly very simple. From the 1970s, these real robots usually had a computer "brain." They could make decisions and even think for themselves. Yet computers have not only altered real-life robots, they have also had a huge effect on fictional robots, too.

Drawn by Computer

Computers are now used to create many movies, animations, and video games. All the pictures, scenes, graphics, and other images are computer-generated images, or **CGI**, for short.

CGI is ideal for science fiction and especially for robots. The writers and designers first create a full three-dimensional (3-D) shape of the robot in the computer's memory. Then they program the computer to make the shape bend, turn, run, and perform other actions. They do the same with other computer-generated characters, including people, animals, aliens, and strange inventions based on everyday objects, from talking toothbrushes to animated rockets.

▼ The Iron Giant *film (1999) used computer animation programs specially written for it. The film was based on a story by writer Ted Hughes, in which a huge metal robot strikes up a friendship with a young boy.*

HAL 9000

*One of the creepiest and most sinister robots in fiction is HAL 9000 from 2001: A Space Odyssey. HAL is an astonishingly advanced computer "brain" on board **deep-space** explorer craft Discovery. As a computer, it is not really a robot. However, HAL takes over the craft's **sensors**, machinery, and other systems, so it can detect what is going on around it and also carry out actions. So it turns into an actual robot. HAL is usually shown in the movie as a simple camera eye. It tries to kill the astronauts on board, but one surviving astronaut takes out HAL's circuits one by one until it "dies."*

Human and Robot Costars

More complicated films combine CGI robots with human actors in the same scene. Usually the actors are filmed in front of a colored background, for example, plain blue. The computer detects the color blue and replaces it with the CGI background, complete with robots and other characters. Once the human characters have been put into the scene, the animators can change the computer-generated parts in any way they like, so it all looks like one scene.

▶▶ *Both robots and cyborgs are human shaped (androids) and human sized, so they can be played by real people in costumes. In Robocop, the hero of the title is played by Peter Weller (see also page 15).*

Goodies, Baddies, and Funnies

Imagining what robots look like and giving them super powers is part of the fun for their creators. Fictional robots also allow their creators to explore whether robots should be good or bad, heroes or villains, nice or nasty.

Nasty Robots

Often, we can see whether robots are goodies or baddies just by looking at them. Nasty robots tend to be dark in color, with a scary-looking, sharp-edged design. If they have a face, then usually the eyes glare and the mouth frowns. If they speak, the voice is deep and snarling. Sometimes these bad 'bots are shaped like animals which many people fear, such as snakes, spiders, and crocodiles. The battle droids in *Star Wars* are examples, with their menacing, skull-like faces.

▶▶ *Marvin the Paranoid Android's face is simple and strange, yet it gives the impression of being glum and depressed. This helps define its personality.*

Nice Robots

Friendly or likeable robots tend to be lighter colored and with a softer appearance. If they look like animals, these are usually familiar creatures that people like, such as cute puppies, chatty parrots, or cuddly teddy bears. The face is big eyed and smiling, and the voice is calm and soothing.

Comedy Robots

Robots are sometimes used to make people smile and laugh. One example was Marvin the Paranoid Android from *The Hitchhiker's Guide to the Galaxy* books, TV series, and films. If you are paranoid, you think that everything and everyone is against you. Marvin was at least 50,000 times more intelligent than a human, yet was always bored and fed up, although funny at the same time. It insisted that the best conversation it ever had was 40 million years ago, with a coffee-making machine.

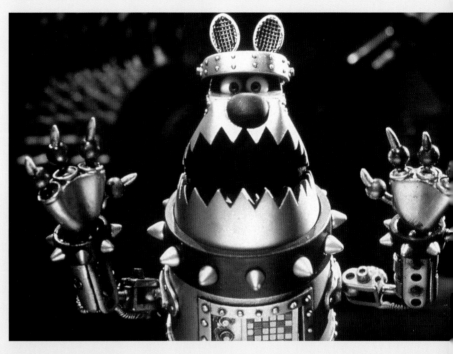

Preston the evil robotic dog appears in Wallace and Gromit's A Close Shave *(1995). Its dark, sinister eyes, fierce teeth, and metal claws suggest that it's the film's baddie.*

Many kinds of battle droids appear in Star Wars *films. Most are robot soldiers that resemble faceless human skeletons. Because they lack identity and character, no one cares if they die.*

ROBOT SUPERSTAR

Twiki

The child-sized robot Twiki, from the TV series Buck Rogers in the 25th Century *broadcast during the 1970s and 1980s, was Buck's friend and helper. When Buck ran into trouble, Twiki often rescued him with lighthearted fun. Twiki's catchphrase was "bidi-bidi-bidi," which was sometimes said for no obvious reason. The robot was played by a very short actor called Felix Silla, who wore a seven-piece suit. Its lines were spoken by Mel Blanc, who has recorded voice-overs for dozens of cartoon stars, including Bugs Bunny, Daffy Duck, and Sylvester the Cat.*

Robots with Feelings and Emotions

Early stories about robots portrayed many of them as simple, unthinking machines. They may have had ray guns and terrific strength, but they carried out only a few tasks and always obeyed their masters. They could not feel emotions or make complex decisions. The rise of "thinking" computers and **artificial intelligence** in the real world gave fiction writers new ideas for their imaginary robots.

David, a robot "mecha" boy, his robotic cuddly toy Teddy, and "mecha" friend Joe stick together and help each other through many emotional moments in AI: Artificial Intelligence.

A Robot with Feelings

In the 2001 movie *AI: Artificial Intelligence*, the main character, David, is a humanlike robot boy or "mecha" (mechanical) who can feel great love. It becomes completely devoted to its human "mother," but it is abandoned in a forest with its robot teddy bear. David discovers that it is not human; it is one of many mechas. This part of the story looks at whether robots should be aware of themselves as robots.

Longing to Be Human

In the forest, David remembers the story of Pinocchio in which a wooden puppet boy thinks that, if it can turn into a real boy, its mother will return its love. David wants to do this and searches for the Blue Fairy who can make him human. But the Blue Fairy does not exist. *AI: Artificial Intelligence* has many sad moments and some happy ones. The complicated character of David, and the plot's many twists and turns, are an example of how robot stories have changed since they were first written 50 years before.

▶▶ *The power of lightning is often used in fiction. It brings sewn-together dead bodies to life in the* Frankenstein *stories (right), and gives robots such as Johnny 5 humanlike awareness and feelings (below).*

DO YOU KNOW?

(ROBOTS DO)

Johnny 5

The 1986 movie Short Circuit *told how robot soldier Number 5 was hit by a power surge during a thunderstorm. Its programs were disrupted, and it wandered away to a chance meeting with a human, Stephanie, who became its friend. Gradually Number 5 realized that the electricity surge had turned it into a real human. It took the name Johnny 5 and decided that it would not be a soldier programmed to kill people. In the story, it is often not clear whether Johnny 5 is still a robot or has become a living being.*

Robot or Human?

Fiction can combine robots with living beings or organisms, especially humans. This involves the science of **cybernetics**, which is the study of how things happen and are controlled, for example, by sensors and **feedback**. The results are cybernetic organisms or cyborgs.

Cylons

The Cylons were several kinds of robots in the Battlestar Galactica television series. Some looked like human-shaped machines, while others looked exactly like people, even with living flesh on the outside. People argue about whether they should be called robots, or cyborgs, or have some other name, such as cybernauts.

Ultimate Space Explorers

The word cyborg was invented in 1960 to describe an imaginary part-human, part-mechanical, part-electronic being for exploring deep space. This being would be tougher and less likely to become ill than a human, yet more intelligent and able to adapt than a robot. In the 1970s, there were TV series with this theme, including *The Six Million Dollar Man* with Lee Majors as cyborg Steve Austin, and Lindsay Wagner as *The Bionic Woman* Jaimie Sommers.

In fiction, cyborgs are usually shown as having both living flesh and artificial parts. Often they have personalities and intelligence, which is part human and part robot. These **characteristics** allow their writers to ask questions about the differences between humans and machines.

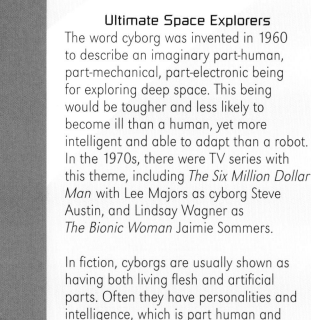

◀◀ *The hero of Six Million Dollar Man was an astronaut whose body cost six million dollars to rebuild after a terrible accident. His robotic parts included two legs, his right arm, and his left eye.*

Movie Villains

In the long-running *Star Trek* programs and movies, the ultimate villains are the Borg. Their saying is "Resistance is futile," and they present a massive threat to humans, **Vulcans**, **Klingons**, **Romulans**, and many other types of beings in the *Star Trek* universe. The Borg operate in one massive intelligent network. What happens to one individual is instantly known to all of them, and they all share knowledge and make decisions.

 *In Star Trek, the Borg (cyborgs) attack and take over all the life-forms and technology they encounter. They add anything useful to themselves and destroy the rest.*

 As well as fighting daleks (see page 11), Doctor Who has fought long-running battles with the Cybermen. These were originally living beings who added more and more mechanical and robotic parts to their bodies.

ROBO-FUTURE

Are Cyborgs Likely?

*Some people today have bodies which are partly **"bionic,"** or which combine living and artificial mechanical parts. They might have metal and plastic joints, heart pacemakers, pins and plates in their bones, plastic tubes for blood vessels, and even microchips in an eye or ear to help sight or hearing. Will medical science ever produce true cyborgs? Most experts would say probably not for a very long time yet.*

When Robots Are Stars

Did you know that a machine can become a world-famous celebrity? That has happened to several robot characters over the years in books, comics, cartoons, and films. People talk about them, mimic their voices and actions, and use their sayings and catchphrases. Sometimes their human creators do not intend for the robot to be the main star. But the audience decides what is successful.

Robot with a Catchphrase

In the science fiction movie *Flight of the Navigator*, made in 1986, a young boy named David is taken for a ride in an alien craft. He travels so fast that, according to the laws of science, time passes very slowly. When he returns what seems like a few hours later, it is eight years later on Earth. The robot spacecraft Max from this story became a great hit, with its fast-moving eye on a stalk and its funny lines, including the catchphrase, "Compliance!"

▼ *In* Flight of the Navigator, *young David can communicate with the robotic spacecraft Max by thinking, and the two become good friends.*

Scary Villains

Far more frightening were the Terminator robotic cyborgs. In the 1984 film *The Terminator*, a T-800 Terminator robot was sent back from the future. Its task was to kill the mother of someone who founded a group of people that resisted takeover by robots. This robot was played by actor Arnold Schwarzenegger, and it was so lifelike that it even bled when it was hurt.

Both T-800 and HAL 9000 from *2001: A Space Odyssey* feature in a list of the top 50 movie villains of all time. The characters were voted for by people who belong to the American Film Institute (AFI). In T-800's second movie, it becomes good, and so it also has a place in the list of the AFI's top 50 heroes.

▶▶ *Before Arnold Schwarzenegger went into politics, one of his many film roles was as the Terminator cyborg with its catchphrase, "Hasta la vista, baby" (See you later, friend).*

Robots in Action■

MEANINGS AND MESSAGES

The computer-animated film *Robots* (2005) features a cast of robots in Robot City, with many action sequences, chases, and similar scenes. The hero Rodney tries to mend old robots instead of sending them to the Chop Shop to be melted down. Like many films featuring robots, there are messages and meanings for people in the real world. For example, we should try to mend or recycle machines and devices, rather than just throw them away and buy new ones. ■

Future Fiction

Every year, writers and other creative people invent new fictional robots. The only limits are their imaginations. Scientific advances and issues in the real world spark ideas, for example, new knowledge about how our brains think, the latest supercomputers, terrorism, the threat of illegal drugs, the Internet, new diseases, and **global warming**.

Robot Hall of Fame

The Robot Hall of Fame is at Carnegie Mellon Science Center in Pittsburgh, Pennsylvania. It honors real and fictional robots that have inspired designers, engineers, and advances in technology. About half are fictional, including R2-D2, C-3PO, HAL 9000, Robbie the Robot, Astro Boy, David, Gort, Maria, T-800 Terminator, as well as Huey, Dewey, and Louie, and Star Trek's Data. Which ones do you think should be future members?

Love Story

An award-winning film in 2008 starred the small robot Waste Allocation Load Lifter, Earth-Class or WALL-E. In this tale from the future, Earth is so polluted and covered with waste that all humans have left. WALL-E meets and falls in love with the advanced robot probe EVE, sent back to look for plant life. The filmmakers' challenge was to convey the robots' thoughts, using only simple actions and a few electronic sounds.

SOLAR CHARGE LEVEL

WALL·E

◄◄ *By altering WALL-E's camera "eyes" very slightly, the filmmakers gave the waste-collecting robot different expressions.*

Themes that Last Forever

The long-running *Transformers* series began in the 1980s with toys, TV cartoons, and animated movies. There are two main groups: Autobots, who are nice and led by Optimus Prime; and the nasty Decepticons, led by their chief Megatron. In the 2000s, the Transformers were updated with the latest computer special effects, but the basic storylines go back a long way. Doubtless they will inspire stories of future fictional robots with their long-lasting themes of love versus hate, freedom versus control, rich versus poor, greed versus giving, and good versus evil.

▶▶ *Bumblebee is one of the smaller junior Transformers, always wanting to impress the larger Autobots. It transforms into a Volkswagen VW Beetle car.*

ROBOT SUPERSTAR

Robo-Duo

*A long time ago, in a **galaxy** far, far away, were C-3PO and R2-D2 of Star Wars. C-3PO was a suit worn by actor Anthony Daniels, who also spoke the words added at a later time. Trashcan-sized R2-D2 was sometimes a radio-controlled model and sometimes with a person inside —Kenny Baker, just 44 inches (112 cm) tall. R2-D2's beeping sounds were created by electronic equipment.*

Glossary

amputee
A person (or animal) who has had a body part removed, either by accident or during a planned operation, such as an ear, finger, hand, or leg.

android
A robot or similar machine designed to resemble a human body, usually with a face, arms, body, and legs.

animator
A person who produces animations, or moving images, such as cartoons, videos, and movies, usually either drawing them by hand or making them on a computer.

artificial intelligence
The intelligence of machines, which are usually computer based. These machines may have the power to think, reason, and remember, so they seem to respond as people do.

bionic
A combination of biological or living parts and nonliving ones such as mechanical and electronic devices.

CGI
Stands for computer-generated images. Images, pictures, and views produced or generated by a computer rather than existing in real life.

characteristics
Features or qualities, such as a particular way of thinking or behaving, or body parts made in a certain way.

computer animation
Animations, or moving images, such as cartoons, videos, and movies, that are produced on a computer.

cybernetics
The science of how and why events happen and are controlled, such as how machines work and how they are organized and run. For example, machines might be monitored by sensors and by using feedback (see below).

cyborg
A being that is part living and part nonliving, usually with some mechanical and electrical parts.

deep space
Space that is far away from Earth, usually outside the Solar System (our Sun and its group of eight planets with their moons).

digital special effects
Special effects (see page 31) that are made, using digital equipment. In digital special effects, everything—including pictures, colors, shapes, and sounds—is represented by groups of numbers.

feedback
Information gathered from sensors, monitors, measurers, and similar devices. The information is sent to a control center to help control a machine or device and to keep it running properly.

frames
Single pictures, scenes, or other images in a sequence, which are shown one after the other very quickly, so they appear to merge together and show movement and action.

galaxy
A giant group of many millions of stars that are relatively close together in a clump, surrounded by vast regions of truly empty space.

global warming
The gradual heating up of the Earth's surface. This is happening because there are growing amounts of some gases in the atmosphere, especially carbon dioxide, which is produced by burning fossil fuels and other fuels.

Klingons
Humanlike beings in the *Star Trek* books, TV programs, and movies. Klingons come from the planet Qo'noS (Kronos), and they start by being enemies of Earth, but usually they end up on the same side. They prefer to solve problems by wars and fighting rather than peaceful discussions.

Romulans

Humanlike beings in the *Star Trek* books, TV programs, and movies. They come from the planets Romulus and Remus, and they are usually enemies of Earth. Sometimes they join up to fight a common enemy such as the Borg. They are generally sneaky, cunning, and not to be trusted.

satellite

An object that goes around, or orbits, another object. The moon is a natural satellite of Earth. Sometimes the word is used to mean man-made objects rather than natural ones.

science fiction

Made-up or imagined stories, that are based on today's scientific knowledge.

sensors

Devices that detect and measure something, such as a camera for light, a microphone for sound, or a magnetometer for magnetic forces.

special effects

Pictures, scenes or images, and also sounds that do not exist in real life, but are created by artists or computer experts.

voice-over

The speech or other voice sounds of a video or movie, which are added after the film has been made.

Vulcans

Humanlike beings in the *Star Trek* books, TV programs, and movies. Vulcans come from the planet Vulcan and are very clever. They think mainly using reason and logic, figuring out events step-by-step. Vulcans try to suppress or think past emotions such as happiness or anger.

Further Reading

Allman, Toney. *The Nexi Robot*. Chicago: Norwood House Press, 2010.

Gifford, Clive. *Robots*. New York: Atheneum, 2008.

Piddock, Charles. *Future Tech: from Personal Robots to Motorized Monocylces*. Washington, D.C.: National Geographic, 2009.

Ferrari, Mario. *Building Robots with LEGO Mindstorms NXT*. Rockland: Syngress, 2007.

Hyland, Tony. *Film and Fiction Robots*. North Mankato: Smart Apple Media, 2008.

Web Sites

Robots in Film: A Complete Illustrated History
This site contains 100 examples of robots, androids, and cyborgs which have appeared in the movies since 1907.
http://www.filmsite.org/robotsinfilm.html

Robot World News
Robot World News covers the top news stories on robotics, artificial intelligence and related areas, but it also has more fun information on robots.
http://www.robotworldnews.com/robots4u.html

Robot Video Clips
Robot Video Clips of all kinds of robots in action.
http://www.robotclips.com/

Robot Wars
In the popular Robot Wars competitions, teams strive to improve robots of all kinds, not just for battle—see especially the SAFETY page.
http://www.ukrobotwars.com/mains.htm

Index